Old South Texas

The Past in Photographs

VOLUME II

By Murphy Givens

Published by the

Corpus Christi Caller-Times

An E.W. Scripps Company

Caller.com

Corpus Christi Central Library

North Beach, c. 1913
Bathing in the bay.

Copyright 2003 Corpus Christi Caller-Times ● All rights reserved. ● ISBN 0-9614752-2-6 ● First Edition
Published by the Corpus Christi Caller-Times. Printed by Golden Banner Press Inc.

Old South Texas

Corpus Christi, c. 1908
This young girl was trying out an early model tricycle. She was either wearing a very unusual hat or it was part of the background scene.

Murphy Givens Collection

Table of Contents

Seaside Hotel 16, 17, 22-23
Camp Scurry 38-39
Oil, gas. 41, 56-57
Nueces Bay Causeway. 42-43
Port of Corpus Christi 48-49, 78, 81, 123
Seawall. 84-85
Naval Air Station 89, 91, 96
World War II 88-97
Box 13 scandal. 106-107
King Ranch 112-115
Duke of Duval 144-147
Homeport. 150-151

Foreword
and
Acknowledgments

The encouraging reception given "Old Corpus Christi: The Past in Photographs," published in 2002, inspired this second effort, "Old South Texas." This book is a continuation of that book, except that this one has a broader scope to bring in photos of towns and cities around Corpus Christi. The intent is the same — to show the richness and variety of the history of South Texas through photographs.

It's hard to look at photos of times gone by and not find subjects of interest. But this is not a study of history; it's more like snapshots of history. Still, they do tell us a good deal about the past.

The plan for this book was simple. We started choosing photos from around the turn of the 20th century working forward, but keeping in mind that as we got closer to our own time, the photographs would lose much of their historical value and interest. Photos of our times will be more valuable for some future book assembler.

Last year's book went from the 1840s until the building of the Harbor Bridge in 1959. This book begins in 1900 and ends with a photo of Mary Rhodes in 1997. We are covering some of the same ground, but with different photos and a wider perspective.

The images were chosen for their simplicity as well as their historical value. Many of these photos carry the credit line of William Frederick "Doc" McGregor, a chiropractor who photographed many thousands of South Texas scenes with freshness and clarity, and without artifice. Doc McGregor's photos seem to entrap the decisive moment. They were made of the moment, and for the moment; we don't suppose they were made with any idea of them acquiring historical value. But they have. Doc McGregor's photos are now in a prized collection at the Corpus Christi Museum of Science and History; they offer an accurate visual record of the history of South Texas.

Putting this book together was made easier by the gracious and unstinting help of Patricia Murphy of the Corpus Christi Museum of Science and History, and Herb Canales and Laura Garcia of the Corpus Christi Central Library, who gave me access to their repository of old photos.

This book has been a learning process for me, and I hope it is for others. If you learn something about where you live, where you came from, where your people came from, then you learn a great many things about yourself.

— *Murphy Givens*

Old South Texas

Corpus Christi Central Library

Mesquite Street, c. 1900
On this panel of grand jury members on the courthouse steps was Calvin J. Allen (fourth from left, bottom, holding hat). Allen owned a 5,000-acre cattle ranch in the Nuecestown area, 12 miles from Corpus Christi on the Nueces River. He convinced railroad officials in 1909 to run their tracks through his ranch rather than Nuecestown, a few miles away. He donated land for a town — Calallen.

South Bluff, c. 1900
Among those identified on the steps of Dr. A.G. Heaney's office and home were Mrs. Heaney, Bessie Almond, Bessie Brooks, Josie Almond and Mrs. Will Wright. Dr. Heaney came to Corpus Christi in 1884; he admitted the first patient to Spohn Sanitarium when it opened on North Beach in 1905. His son Harry G. Heaney also was a longtime practicing physician in Corpus Christi.

Corpus Christi, c. 1900
Around the turn of the 20th century, the Corpus Christi Kids baseball team was one of the hottest teams in the state, until it ran into a team from Lockhart that had attracted a professional pitcher. The next year, the Kids imported a semi-pro pitcher of their own and beat Lockhart. The Kids here include: (left to right, bottom row) Ed Gollihar, pitcher; Joe Mireur, catcher and captain; Jonas Weil, pitcher; (second row) Dave Segrest, third base; John Dossel, second base; Dr. H.H. Segrest, manager; Moise Weil, shortstop, and Warren Chapman, third base; (top row) Tim Williams, right field; Mike Mitchell, center field; and Charles Reuthinger, left field.

Old South Texas

Corpus Christi Central Library

Carancahua, c. 1900
Students at Corpus Christi's old Central High School, built in the 1890s. A new high school was built on this site in 1911. While construction was in progress, students attended a temporary school on Staples that they called the "chicken coop" school.

Old South Texas

Chaparral Street, c. 1900
A circus took elephants on parade in downtown Corpus Christi around the turn of the 20th century.

Old South Texas

Caller-Times Archives

Robstown, c. 1902

No. 101, a coal-burner, was brought to Corpus Christi from Oklahoma in 1902. It worked out of Robstown hauling supplies for construction of the railroad line to Brownsville. As the St. Louis, Brownsville & Mexico Railroad line moved south, new towns sprang up. The line reached Kingsville in May 1904. The "Brownie" opened up the Valley to rail transportation, and development soon followed. Every town between Corpus Christi and Brownsville can date its beginning to the building of the "Brownie."

Old South Texas

Caller-Times Archives

Off Tarpon (Port Aransas), c. 1905

A fleet of rowboats was being towed to the "tarpon grounds" near Port Aransas. Around the turn of the 20th Century, tarpon fishermen went out in small boats, often as far as five miles out into the Gulf. They fished with heavy rods and straight-handled reels, which required brute strength to bring in a trophy-sized tarpon. But tarpon were caught in large numbers, as well as redfish and speckled trout. At this time, Port Aransas was named Tarpon. The name was changed to Port Aransas when the town was incorporated in 1911.

Bayfront, c. 1900
A string of trout, the product of a family fishing trip, was displayed on a bayfront fishing pier.

Corpus Christi, c. 1908
Robert Ritter (owner of Ritter's Racket Store) and his son Armin went duck hunting on Poenisch Lake, where Oso Golf Course is today.

Caller-Times Archives

Port Aransas, 1900
When Port Aransas was called Tarpon, at the turn of the 20th century, a favorite hangout was Cline's Restaurant, owned by Edward Cline. He also ran a ship chandlery, a hotel and a hunting and fishing guide center. After Cline's operation was destroyed in a hurricane, he moved to Flour Bluff. The 1916 and 1919 storms wiped him out again, but he built back. He died in 1929.

Kingsville, 1904

Charles Flato Jr., one of the founders of Kingsville, was standing in front of the shed where railroad workers came for their meals. It was called the "eat shed." On the left was the "sleep tent" and on the right was Kingsville's water well and cistern. Flato moved from Shiner to Kingsville that year and opened a lumberyard.

Caller-Times Archives

Corpus Christi, c. 1905
Corpus Christi heiress Clara Driscoll was called the "Savior of the Alamo" after she bought the property surrounding the historic old building in 1903 to save it from commercial exploitation. After Robert Driscoll's death in 1929, she succeeded her brother as president of Corpus Christi Bank and Trust. She built the Robert Driscoll Hotel on Upper Broadway in 1942. When she died in 1945, she left the Driscoll fortune to build and operate the Driscoll Foundation Children's Hospital.

Harriet Tillman/Poenisch Family Archives

Corpus Christi, c. 1905
Robert Poenisch. One of the city's oldest bayfront parks — Poenisch Park, at 5700 Ocean Drive — was named for the Poenisch family, natives of Dresden, Germany, who located in Corpus Christi in 1889 to farm what is now the city's Southside. Robert Poenisch helped develop the area by building a subdivision off Ocean Drive in the 1930s. He set aside a site at Ocean and Claremore for a park, which bears the family name.

Mesquite Street, c. 1905

Artesian Park, with its bandstand, was a social center for Corpus Christi for decades. Band concerts and political events were held in the park. The artesian well that gave the park its name was drilled in 1845 by Zachary Taylor's troops. The well was abandoned. Town founder Henry Kinney tried to drill another well on the site, but quit when it was half completed. He gave the well, and the land around it to the city, if the city would finish the job. The water had a smelly sulfur content, redolent of rotten eggs. It was later bottled and sold as a health tonic. It was said to cure catarrh, rheumatism, stomach ailments, and baldness.

Water Street, c. 1905
Women gather under the canopy of salt cedars in the Salt Cedar Garden at the Seaside Hotel. The hotel was located at the corner of Water Street and Taylor (where the back end of One Shoreline Plaza is today). The hotel was enlarged from the old Dix house, built before the Civil War. The hotel, with its salt cedar grove, was destroyed in the 1919 storm.

Water Street, 1907

The dining room of the Seaside Hotel. Oilman Jack Innis bought the old John Dix home on Water Street and converted it to the Seaside Hotel. It was famous for its food. Items featured from a 1908 menu included "Stuffed Red Head Duck with French Dressing" and "Broiled Oysters a la Maitre d'Hotel."

Corpus Christi Central Library

Old Corpus Christi

Caller-Times Archives

Rockport, c. 1905

The Aransas Hotel (later renamed the Del Mar Hotel) was built on the waterfront in 1889. It was said to be the largest wooden hotel in the United States; its central dining room, with no visible support, was called a wonder. The hotel was a favorite with tourists who would take the San Antonio and Aransas Pass Railroad (SAAP) to Rockport, which was just beginning to be known as a coastal resort. The hotel burned on March 6, 1919 — six months before the 1919 hurricane struck.

Aransas Pass, c. 1910

The gabled, four-story Bayview Hotel was first named the Hoyt Hotel, after the original owner, A. Marie Hoyt. It was built in 1892, but closed a few years later. It was supposed to be first prize in a land-buying lottery in 1909. But because lotteries were illegal, what had been a phony auction became a real one when government officials showed up. The Bayview eventually sold at the auction for $16,500. It was torn down in 1918.

Caller-Times Archives

Murphy Givens Collection

Rockport, c. 1910

The Bailey Pavilion (center) was built on a wharf in front of the Del Mar Hotel. On the left was the Coleman Fulton Pasture Company wharf. The Bailey Pavilion was the center of social activity, featuring plays and variety acts; it was famous for its dance parties. The 1919 hurricane ripped away the pavilion and left much of it at the corner of Live Oak and Market streets. Most of Rockport's waterfront was destroyed in the storm.

Sinton, 1910
Attending a meeting of the Sinton Ladies Club were (top row, left to right): Mrs. W.E. Hopkins, Kingsville; Miss Lizzie McGloin, Mrs. J.G. Cook, Mrs. Jess Neill, and Mrs J.I. Knox, all of Sinton. Bottom row: Mrs. Arthur Cross, Waco; Mrs. J.M. Lisler, Long Beach, Calif.; Mrs. Abbie Craft, El Campo; Mrs. Mable Atkinson, and Mrs. Sam Nelson, both of Bishop. Sinton, founded in 1886, was named for David Sinton, a Cincinnati businessman who made a fortune selling pig iron to the federal government during the Civil War. He was the majority stockholder in the Coleman-Mathis Pasture Co.

Corpus Christi Central Library

Staples Street, 1910
Corpus Christi High School's football team of 1910. High school students at this time were attending school in a temporary frame building, known as the "chicken coop" school, at Staples and Park while waiting for the construction of a new high school building. It was completed the following year.

Corpus Christi Central Library

Corpus Christi Central Library

Water Street, 1908

A large crowd gathered in front of the Salt Cedar Garden at the Seaside Hotel. William Jennings Bryan (baldheaded man with cane, center front) attended the Inland Waterway Convention in Corpus Christi on Nov. 17, 1908. This was two weeks after Bryan lost his third bid to become president. He was defeated by William Howard Taft, 314 to 169 electoral votes. Taft himself came to visit Corpus Christi in 1909. Bryan that year bought property in Mission and became a regular Winter Texan.

Old South Texas

Corpus Christi Central Library

Robstown, 1909
The George H. Paul company brought in trainloads of "homeseekers" from Missouri, Kansas, Nebraska, Iowa and other Midwestern states. They would be taken in buggies to see farm sites; in this case, carved from the Driscoll Ranch. Paul's first trainload of prospective buyers arrived in Robstown in 1907.

Corpus Christi Bay, c. 1910
The steamer Pilot Boy was loaded with "homeseekers" brought to the area by land promoter George H. Paul. Paul never tried to sell land on Sunday. He would take those buyers who wanted to attend church to Corpus Christi for services, and others would be taken on an excursion across the bay and into the gulf on the Pilot Boy. The Pilot Boy went down just north of the Aransas Pass jetties in the storm of 1916.

Corpus Christi Central Library

Old South Texas

Corpus Christi, c. 1911

U.S. Heinley of Denver (front seat) and his brothers V.S. and Earl purchased the Corpus Christi & Interurban Railway Co. from Daniel Hewett in 1911. The Heinleys added three new cars to the line and built their own power plant, which ran on Mexican oil (the discovery of oil in the Corpus Christi area was two decades away). The Heinleys sold out in 1914 to a syndicate from Philadelphia. Corpus Christi's last electric trolley car made its final run on Jan. 31, 1931.

Corpus Christi Central Library

Tiger Street, 1910

These men, presumably the investors, gathered at the San Antonio & Aransas Pass Depot for the arrival of the first railroad car of the new Corpus Christi & Interurban Railway Co. Corpus Christi had steam-powered and mule-powered streetcars dating back to the late 1880s, but this was the first electric streetcar. The new streetcar line was operated by Daniel Hewett.

Corpus Christi Central Library

Chaparral Street, c. 1912

This street scene was about 1912, judging by the streetcar rails, which were laid in 1910. The white building on the left was Corpus Christi National Bank, on the northwestern corner of Chaparral at Schatzel.

Corpus Christi Central Library

Old South Texas

Ocean Drive, 1910

The buggy was traveling south on Ocean Drive, past Airline Road. The house on the right was W.A. "Farmer" Clark's. Down the road on the left was the Aberdeen Baptist Church. Ocean Drive began in 1904 when property owners petitioned the city to extend Water Street along the beach to the old Alta Vista Hotel at Three-Mile Point. The homeowners' petition said the new street would give the city "a beautiful driveway, and make some desirable building sites accessible."

Caller-Times Archives

Caller-Times Archives

Carancahua, c. 1912

Corpus Christi's first high school building built for the purpose was constructed in 1911. It cost the school district $85,000 and was called "the brick palace." It served as the high school until a new high school was built in 1929 (which later became Miller High School). The brick palace became the Northside Junior High School in 1929.

Corpus Christi Central Library

San Diego, c. 1910

Duval County's first courthouse, built in 1878, was destroyed by fire on Aug. 14, 1914, when Archer Parr, the first "Duke of Duval," was being investigated by the state attorney general's office for corruption. It was suspected that the courthouse was burned to destroy incriminating records.

Old South Texas

Caller-Times Archives

Aransas Pass, 1909
Homeseekers crowded Aransas Pass for the Burton & Danforth town lot auction. The tent was set up to house the crowd on auction day. Land agents E.O. Burton and A.H. Danforth promoted Aransas Pass as a Houston in the making, a "deep-water boom town." Some 6,000 lots were sold by the agents. Many of those lots were sold again, in 1951, at a sheriff's sale to collect delinquent taxes owed by out-of-state buyers.

Leopard at Waco, c. 1910
Saloon proprietor Ben Grande behind the bar with one customer in front of the bar. The Ben Grande was an institution in Corpus Christi, dating back to the early 1890s when it was established by Frank Grande Sr. The saloon patio was famous for its cockfights. The building was torn down in 1950.

Corpus Christi Central Library

Corpus Christi, 1911

The waiting room at one of Corpus Christi's three depots. Corpus Christi at this time had railroad passenger service provided by the Texas Mexican Railway, the St. Louis, Brownsville and Mexico Railroad, and the San Antonio and Aransas Pass Railroad (SAAP), soon to be absorbed by Missouri Pacific. The Tex-Mex Depot was on Railroad Avenue, where Trinity Towers is today; the SAAP Depot was on Tiger (an extension of Broadway) at Belden; and the Union Depot (for the "Brownie" line) was on the other side of Staples, between Comanche and Kinney. Daily passenger service in Corpus Christi ended on June 30, 1962 when Missouri-Pacific's last passenger train left the depot.

Old South Texas

North Beach, 1913
She was wearing a "bathing costume" for a dip in the bay; there were no suntans in those days. In the 1920s, shorter swimsuits became fashionable for both men and women.

Corpus Christi Central Library

North Beach, c. 1916
A buoy washed up on the beach in the 1916 storm.

Caller-Times Archives

Old South Texas

Robstown, c. 1912
The Brendle Gin, Robstown's first cotton gin, was built in 1910-1911.

Wooldridge Road, 1913
Herman and Bertha Poenisch and family tried out their first car, a Ford "touring car," in front of the family home on Wooldridge. Since the roads were graded dirt, when it rained the Ford was parked and they would switch back to a team and wagon.

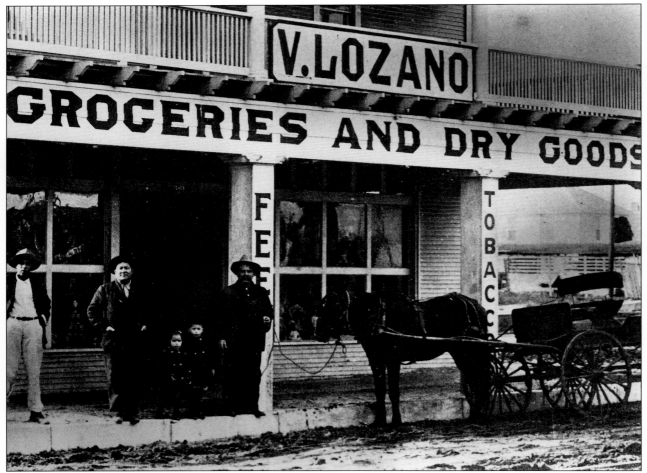

Staples Street, 1914
Vicente Lozano's grocery and dry goods store was built in 1913 at Staples and Agnes. In 1900, Lozano built his first store in the 100 block of North Chaparral. The adults in the photo (left to right) were Daniel McCarthy, Mrs. Lozano's brother; Vicente Lozano; and Alberto Longoria. The children in the photo were Paula, 3, and Gabe Lozano, 5. Gabe Lozano was appointed mayor of Corpus Christi in 1977.

Corpus Christi, 1899
Vicente Lozano and his wife Elmira McCarthy shortly after they were married. Lozano worked for John Mircovich in the John Two Brothers Grocery and Saloon on North Chaparral. Lozano soon became a successful businessman; he owned an early grocery store and later had an interest in KCCT Radio and KVDO, Corpus Christi's first TV station. His son Gabe Lozano Sr. was mayor in 1977-'78.

Port Aransas, 1915

A day's catch of king mackerel on display.

Port Aransas, c. 1915

Fishermen displayed their prize trophy tarpons — one 5-foot-8 and the other 5-foot-10.

Robstown, c. 1915
A "money raising" sale was under way at John Allen Ligon's store. Ligon opened his store soon after he moved from La Grange to Robstown in 1912. He was elected mayor of Robstown in 1928; he died the following year. His son was Ben Allen Ligon, longtime district clerk in Nueces County.

Corpus Christi Central Library

Bayfront, 1916
The 98-foot pleasure boat Japonica, owned by Capt. Andrew Anderson, was damaged and washed aground in the 1916 hurricane. The ship survived to become a popular excursion vessel plying bay waters, with regular runs between Corpus Christi, Port Aransas and Rockport. It burned and sank in the Mississippi River in 1946.

Caller-Times Archives

Corpus Christi, 1916
Power crews worked to repair downed lines after the 1916 hurricane, which made landfall near Corpus Christi on Aug. 18. The storm destroyed boats in the harbor and piers on the bayfront, including Loyd's Pavilion, the Ladies Pavilion, and the Seaside Pavilion Hotel pier.

Old South Texas

Corpus Christi, 1917

The U.S. Army's World War I-era training camp built in Corpus Christi in 1916 was officially called Camp Scurry, but most people in Corpus Christi called it "the Soldiers' Camp." It was located in the area now known as Del Mar. The camp had screened and floored tents, wooden mess halls, trenches used for training, and rifle and machine-gun ranges. Two of the men identified here were from Corpus Christi, Thomas Hirsch (left) and Clarence McCandless (third from left).

Corpus Christi Central Library

Lower Broadway at Schatzel, 1917

Military police in a National Guard unit mobilized for national service in World War I. The unit was stationed at Camp Scurry. The photo was taken in front of the Confederate Memorial Fountain, designed by Pompeo Coppini in 1914.

Corpus Christi, 1917

The Second Texas Infantry, stationed at Camp Scurry in World War I, produced what was called the greatest football team in the history of the game. The Second Texas was taking on a team from Camp Travis in a New Year's Day contest. The Second Texas that season ran up a total of 432 points to the opposition's 6.

Old South Texas

Texas Maritime Museum

Rockport, 1919

The Baychester, built at Heldenfels Shipyard in Rockport, was decorated for launching on July 31, 1919. It was one of four ships contracted for the government's Emergency Fleet Corporation. It was built to haul supplies to the American Expeditionary Force fighting in France, but the ship was not finished when the war ended. The wife of President Woodrow Wilson attended the launching and was given the honor of naming the vessel. Heldenfels Shipyard was destroyed two months later in the hurricane of 1919.

Old South Texas

White Point, 1914

This gas well blowout in November 1914 resisted all efforts to bring it under control. Hope of capping the well ended when the gas ignited and the well caught fire. The fire burned for two months and could be smothered only after the tremendous pressure diminished. It was reported that the blowout could be seen and heard for 14 miles. It left a hole 50 feet deep and 150 feet across. The gas pressure at the White Point gasser was estimated to be 60 million cubic feet a day before it was finally choked out. Gas then had no value, but oilmen figured that where there were heavy gas deposits, there was bound to be oil. This blowout intensified the search for oil in the Corpus Christi region.

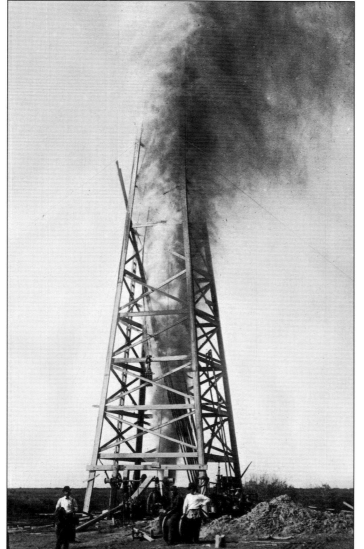

Corpus Christi Central Library

Otto Freier/Corpus Christi Central Library

White Point, 1916

Another gas well blowout in the White Point field on the Rachal Ranch, across Nueces Bay from Corpus Christi. One oilman predicted the area would become the most important discovery field in South Texas. "I expect to see so much activity in the White Point field that a man on one derrick can swap chaws with a fellow on another derrick without much of a stretch."

Old South Texas

Nueces Bay, 1964
The old Nueces Bay railroad trestle was built in 1884 by the San Antonio and Aransas Pass (SAAP) Railroad. It was built of creosoted pilings and outlasted two causeways, the first built in 1914 and the second one in 1921. Use of the railroad trestle was discontinued in 1965 when trains were relocated to Missouri Pacific tracks entering Corpus Christi from the west. The trestle was torn down in 1966.

Corpus Christi Central Library

Old South Texas

Nueces Bay, 1921

Workers were building a trestle-style causeway across Nueces Bay to replace the concrete span that was destroyed in the 1919 storm. This low, narrow wooden bridge served to carry traffic between Corpus Christi and Portland until the first of two concrete causeways was built in 1950.

Corpus Christi Central Library

Nueces Bay, c. 1925

The first causeway connecting Corpus Christi to Portland was an elegant structure made of concrete. It was washed away in the storm of 1919. This second wooden causeway was a temporary bridge built two years later at a cost of $400,000. It was opened to traffic on Oct. 8, 1921.

Caller-Times Archives

South Texas Archives & Special Collections
Jernigan Museum
Texas A&M University-Kingsville

Kingsville, 1925

Some 5,000 people turned out for the cornerstone laying at South Texas State Teachers College on May 21. Gov. Miriam "Ma" Ferguson was the guest of honor and her husband, former governor James Ferguson, delivered the main address. Competition between South Texas cities had been keen to get the college, but Kingsville won out when the Kingsville Town and Development Co. donated 107 acres for a campus site. The college was renamed Texas A&I and is now Texas A&M University-Kingsville.

Old South Texas

Chaparral, c. 1920
W.H. Hull, president of the Corpus Christi Transfer Co., was seated at the desk; behind him was his secretary Ada Edwards. The man standing at left was Oliver Currie; the other man was not identified.

Harbor Island, 1920
The Durham was one of two concrete tankers built on Harbor Island, across from Port Aransas, between 1918 and 1920 by the France & Canada Steamship Co. Port Aransas was chosen as a site for the shipyard because its climate would permit concrete to be poured year-round. The cigar-shaped concrete ships were designed to carry 50,000 barrels of oil. After they were launched in 1920, it was discovered the heavy ships could not navigate, requiring tugs to nurse them along. One sank on the way to Galveston and the other was docked in the Sabine River above Port Arthur for several years.

North Beach, 1920
Pupils of the First Baptist Church Sunday School, wearing bathing caps, on North Beach. Maude Gerhardt (who took the photo) taught the class.

Water Street, c. 1925
School baseball team at the David Hirsch Elementary at 1907 Water Street, next to the Great Chief Camp. The school was closed for six years after it was badly damaged in the 1919 storm. It reopened in 1925 and closed in 1961. The Corpus Christi Museum of Science and History is located on that site today. The school was named for David Hirsch, wool merchant and bank president.

Rose Hill Cemetery, 1925
Ku Klux Klan members turned out for the burial of W. F. "Wildfire" Johnston, who had been a candidate for sheriff in 1922. The KKK was active in the Corpus Christi area in the 1920s. A local Klan leader, Fred Roberts, was shot to death in front of a store on Railroad Avenue on Oct. 22, 1922. The shooting led to the indictment for murder of Nueces County Sheriff Frank Robinson and his deputy Joe Acebo. They were acquitted in a trial in Laredo, but Robinson, fearing Klan retaliation, fled to Mexico, where he lived for several years.

North Chaparral, c. 1925
The Metropolitan Café at 617 N. Chaparral was owned and operated by Ben Garza and three partners, who bought the place in 1919. Garza became head of a group of Hispanics known as Council No. 4 of the Order of Sons of America. This and other Hispanic groups in South Texas merged to become the League of United Latin American Citizens (LULAC). Garza was the first president of LULAC. He closed the café in 1931; he died of tuberculosis in 1937.

Old South Texas

Caller-Times Archives

Bayfront, 1924
Building the wharf and transfer sheds was one of the first stages of construction for the coming Port of Corpus Christi. Old salt flats were dredged for the port's main turning basin. The construction of the port proceeded at a fast pace; less than four years after President Warren Harding signed the Rivers and Harbor Act, which included the authorization, the Port of Corpus Christi was opened.

Caller-Times Archives

Bayfront, 1926

The destroyer USS Borie sailed under the new bascule bridge in port dedication ceremonies on Sept. 14, 1926. The ship later was in one of the most unusual battles in World War II. Near Gibraltar, the Borie rammed a damaged U-boat and the vessels were locked together. German submariners swarmed onto the Borie's deck and the crews fought hand-to-hand, using rifles, pistols, knives and flare guns. The Borie and U-boat 405 were both sunk in the action. The story was the basis for the movie, "The Enemy Below."

Bayfront, 1926

One of the first vessels to dock at the new port was the freighter Ogontz. It was a great day for Corpus Christi when the port opened for commerce, on Sept. 14, 1926. The biggest celebration in the city's history was held, with excursion trains bringing visitors from San Antonio and Houston. Automobiles clogged the roads for miles leading into Corpus Christi.

Murphy Givens Collection

Murphy Givens Collection

Corpus Christi, c. 1925

Robert Driscoll Jr. practiced law in New York City until he returned to South Texas to take over management of the family ranch. He was named president of Corpus Christi National Bank and, in 1923, became chairman of the Nueces County Navigation District, which led to the creation of the Port of Corpus Christi. He died in 1929 after a leg infection resulted in two amputations. On July 7, 1929, Corpus Christi businesses closed their doors for one hour to pay final respects.

Old South Texas

Peoples Street, 1926
The Missouri-Pacific Railroad ticket office was located at 422 Peoples. The Missouri-Pacific Depot was at Oso and Tiger (later renamed West Broadway) streets.

Brownsville Road, 1929
Members of the Corpus Christi Aero Club at its first meeting. The club was founded by Cliff Maus and R.J. Roberts.

Ocean Drive, 1930
A short-lived restaurant was located in a lighthouse-style building outside the city, on Ocean Drive, past the Airline intersection on the way to Ward Island.

Alice, 1931

Looking east, down Main Street, men were congregated in front of the Rex Theater. Alice was known as the "Hub City" because two main highways, 44 and 281, intersected at Alice, and so did two railroad lines, the Texas-Mexican Railway and the Southern Pacific.

South Texas Museum

North Beach, 1930

Harold J. Ross staged a dance marathon at the Crystal Beach Park ballroom on North Beach. The marathon lasted for 31 days before couple #3 (Mary Myers and Tommy Thomas) won when one dancer in the other couple, known as "Watermelon Red," failed to keep his feet moving. For their 31 days of suffering, the winning sore-footed couple took home to Mission $600. Several of the contestants were hospitalized for exhaustion before the grueling contest ended.

Doc McGregor/Corpus Christi Museum of Science and History

Old South Texas

Doc McGregor/Corpus Christi Museum of Science and History

Portland, 1931

The Portland Hotel first opened in December 1891, with more than 100 guests from Corpus Christi, who rode the San Antonio and Aransas Pass (SAAP) train across the bay for the occasion. It closed a few years later. It was reopened in the 1930s as a sanatorium operated, as the sign above says, by Dr. Leon Hemes, specializing in "mechano therapy baths" and "scientific massage."

Waco Street, c. 1930
Lerma Poultry-Eggs may have been a side business of Lerma's Meat Market, which used the same phone number. The firm was no longer listed as being in business by 1933.

South Texas cowboys. J. Frank Dobie in "A Vaquero of the Brush Country" described the cowboy as "a good rider, skilled, observant, alert, resourceful, unyielding, daring, punctilious in a code peculiar to his occupation, and faithful to his trust."

Old South Texas

Up River Road, 1922
The Dunn No. 2 spouted gas, water and mud as it cleared itself out. This was the second gas well on the Dunn land; it was a forerunner of Dunn No. 6, Nueces County's first oil well that came in on Aug. 16, 1930.

Doc McGregor/Corpus Christi Museum of Science and History

Up River Road, 1930
Nueces County's first oil well flowed into pits, while a crowd of interested Corpus Christi citizens looked on. The well was the Saxet Oil and Gas Co.'s No. 6 John Dunn, brought in on Aug. 16, 1930. The discovery signaled the beginning of the oil boom in the Coastal Bend. The No. 6 John Dunn ran dry after producing only 1,440 barrels of oil, but it was the forerunner of oil wells that produced millions of barrels of oil in Nueces County.

1930: The oil era begins

The history of the oil industry in the Corpus Christi area began with the White Point gas blowouts in 1914. The "gassers" across Nueces Bay put on a fiery display of burning gas. Wildcatters knew that where there were heavy gas deposits, there was oil, and they continued to drill. One day in 1930, they were drilling in the Saxet field, on John Dunn's property, when they hit the jackpot on Aug. 16. The *Caller-Times* printed an extra, with a banner head reading: "Dunn No. 6 Near City Comes In As Oil Well." Corpus Christi residents drove out to the field to see the gusher.

Other strikes followed in the Clarkwood area, in the Agua Dulce field, the Saxet West (or Turkey Creek) field, the Sandia field in Jim Wells County, the Plymouth, Taft and Midway fields in San Patricio County, and many more.

The oil boom transformed the Port of Corpus Christi from a small cotton-shipping port to one of the largest ports in the country. The oil boom helped the port to expand, which in turn brought in petrochemical plants. As the port grew, so did the city.

Doc McGregor/Corpus Christi Central Library

Near Taft, 1938

Oilfield workers surveyed a raging fire at a test well three miles south of Taft. A leak in the casing caused the explosion and fire at the Harlan Grimes No. 2 in the Midway field on July 21, 1938. More than 2,000 sacks of cement and cottonseed were pumped into the burning crater in an unsuccessful effort to put out the flames, which continued to burn for several weeks until it burned itself out.

Doc McGregor/Corpus Christi Museum of Science and History

Flour Bluff, 1932

The Don Patricio Causeway to Padre Island, built in 1927, always attracted a line of anglers, who would have to shift from one side to the other when cars appeared. The 1933 hurricane knocked big gaps in the causeway and it was never rebuilt. It was located about one mile south of the present JFK Causeway.

Old South Texas

Pleasure Pier, 1932

With an air of triumphant nonchalance, duck hunters displayed the results of the day's hunting on Nov. 26, 1932. In earlier times, around the turn of the 20th century, redhead ducks were so plentiful they were hunted commercially in the Corpus Christi area and sold for 10 cents each. The state stopped the commercial sale of wild ducks in 1905.

North Chaparral, 1935

Bob Swantner Sr. (of Swantner & Gordon Insurance Agency) stopped by Doc McGregor's studio to show off a buck and turkey he killed. Swantner eventually hunted big game in Africa.

Starr Street, 1931
A panel truck loaded with 300 gallons of smuggled liquor was intercepted by U.S. Customs officers near Sinton. Shown left to right were Cleve Hurst, Robert Heether, John Wolford, Dewey Tom, Joe Jackson, N.A. Miller and Fred Edwards.

Corpus Christi, 1932
Law enforcement officers at an illegal still. Distilleries like this one were common during Prohibition. Welding shops in Corpus Christi turned out cylindrical copper kettles for cooking corn or grain mash. Prohibition agents — revenuers — continually searched for illicit whiskey-making operations, but the illegal spirits still flowed until Prohibition was repealed in 1933.

Old South Texas

Chaparral Street, 1934

The small building next to the Ritz Theater was Jack Brown's woodwork shop. Originally it was the Ranahan home, built of shellcrete in 1853. A federal shell during the bombardment of Corpus Christi in 1862 left a three-foot hole in the front wall. The building was torn down in 1938 to make way for a parking lot. Ed Brennan, a longtime Corpus Christi house-mover, was killed in demolishing the old home when a wall fell on him.

Caller-Times Archives

Port Aransas, 1934

The famous evangelist Aimee Semple McPherson with a string of mackerel she caught while fishing near Port Aransas. She also hooked a five-foot, 78-pound tarpon (bottom). McPherson's fishing guide, Barney Farley, cautioned a reporter to be sure to spell her middle name right: "There's nothing simple about Aimee."

North 19th Street, 1935
Thousands of people attended the South Texas Exposition in 1934, '35 and '36. The annual exposition featured livestock and poultry judging events, crop displays, horse shows, merchant exhibits, floral displays, and entertainment programs. The event that attracted the largest crowd in 1935 was the appearance of radio star (and later governor) 'Pappy' O'Daniel and his Hillbilly Band. The South Texas Exposition was held in a warehouse near the port that had two acres of floor space.

Washington, D.C., 1934
Lyndon B. Johnson sent a signed copy of his portrait to Roy Miller, former mayor of Corpus Christi. Johnson was given the job of personal secretary to Congressman Richard Kleberg in large part because of Miller's recommendation. Miller was Kleberg's campaign manager in the 1931 campaign. LBJ left Kleberg to become state director of the National Youth Administration; then he was elected to Congress.

Old South Texas

Corpus Christi, 1934

During the Great Depression, a café in Corpus Christi prominently displayed the keystone of President Franklin D. Roosevelt's New Deal — the eagle of the National Recovery Administration. The symbol signified the acceptance of a code designed to bring accord between labor and management and to strive to help the national economy recover. Note the menu prices on the wall.

Doc McGregor/Corpus Christi Central Library

Bayfront, 1934
Strollers and fishermen took advantage of fine weather in February for a stroll down Corpus Christi's Pleasure Pier. The Pleasure Pier was built in 1922 and eventually replaced by the city's new seawall and T-Heads. The five buildings that dominated the skyline in 1934 included (from left) the Medical-Professional Building, the Nixon office building, the Plaza Hotel, the Jones Building, and the Nueces Hotel.

Bayfront, 1937
At the end of the Pleasure Pier was a shaded pavilion, where large pleasure boats docked.

Old South Texas

Kingsville, 1935
Young thoroughbreds were shown off at a training session on Oct. 10, 1935, at the Kingsville race track, named for the late Charles Flato Jr. The track was used for many years until it became part of the campus of Texas A&I (now Texas A&M University-Kingsville). Javelina Stadium was built over the old race track.

Caller-Times Archives

Sinton, 1936
A parade in Sinton on April 14 observed the centennial of the founding of San Patricio County. Early Irish settlers took refuge in Victoria during the Texas Revolution, then returned after the battle of San Jacinto. The county was created in 1836, with the town of San Patricio on the Nueces River named the county seat.

Caller-Times Archives

Corpus Christi, 1936
On Nov. 23, work was progressing on the city's new ground-level water reservoir off Caldwell Street. The reservoir was completed early in 1938, helping the city to meet peak water demands in the late afternoon.

Ayers Street, 1937
An aerial view of the rear of Corpus Christi's Wynn Seale Junior High School. Before the school was built in 1935, the site had been leased for growing cotton. Because of the city's rapid growth after the opening of the new port in 1926, the school district was forced to put junior high students on half-day schedules while waiting for the new junior high to be built to help solve the district's growing pains.

Old South Texas

Sarita, 1939
There was no traffic around the Sarita Mercantile Co. and Post Office. The town of Sarita, county seat of Kenedy County, was named for Sarita Kenedy (East), granddaughter of pioneer rancher Mifflin Kenedy. The town of Sarita sits in the middle of four great cattle ranches, La Parra (Kenedy's), King, Armstrong, and Yturria.

Corpus Christi Central Library

Leopard Street, 1937
Pig Stand No. 2 was near the intersection of Leopard and Port. Pig Stand No. 1 was on Chaparral near the bascule bridge.

Corpus Christi Central Library

Caller-Times Archives

Off Corpus Christi Bay, 1936
La Quinta (Spanish for "country house") was built in 1907. President William Howard Taft stayed here when he visited his half-brother, Charles Taft, in 1909. For the president's visit, a nine-hole golf course was constructed and a shell road was built from Gregory, three miles away. The mansion burned in January 1938.

Old South Texas

Doc McGregor/Caller-Times Archives

Port of Corpus Christi, 1936

The Daylite, a converted World War I vessel, relied on two kinds of power. In the ship channel, the vessel used an auxiliary engine; in the Gulf, it hoisted sails for wind power. The Daylite hauled gypsum (an ore used in making plasterboard) from Corpus Christi to Mobile. The gypsum was mined at the old Gyp-Mine near Falfurrias. It was shown here going past the bascule bridge, heading for the bay.

Off Port Aransas, 1937
President Franklin D. Roosevelt (with fishing rod) reeled in this 4-foot, 8-inch tarpon off Port Aransas on May 3. His son Elliott was holding the fish, with fishing guide Barney Farley on the right. FDR landed another tarpon, a 5-foot, 2-inch 77-pounder on May 8. He also caught four kingfish. The president and Elliott sailed to Port Aransas aboard the presidential yacht Potomac for a nine-day fishing vacation. The president visited Port Isabel and Brownsville before returning to Washington.

Port Aransas, 1937
A crowd gathered at Barney Farley's place, hoping to see President Roosevelt. The president during his fishing vacation stayed on the presidential yacht Potomac, anchored off Harbor Island.

Old South Texas

Doc McGregor/Corpus Christi Central Library

S. Staples, 1936

The KC Barbecue Stand, in the 300 block of Staples, was operated by Mrs. Lucille Kohrman. Note the prices: plate lunch, 25 cents with drink, hamburgers five cents, cigarettes 15 cents a pack. Within five years, people in Corpus Christi would be complaining about the increased living costs as a consequence of the boom brought about by the building of the Naval Air Station.

Old South Texas

Caller-Times Archives

Water Street, 1934

Water Street was still on the water, before the bayfront improvement project extended the city into the bay by two blocks. On the left was the First Presbyterian Church, on South Bluff, and in the center was the city's lone skyscraper, the Nixon (later Wilson) Building. On the right is the city's Municipal Wharf.

Old South Texas

Bayfront, 1937
Corpus Christi's Municipal Pier stretched into the bay from Water Street. Just south of the pier was the San Antonio Machine Supply Co. factory (Samsco).

Doc McGregor/Corpus Christi Central Library

Chaparral, 1939
The office and warehouse of the San Antonio Machine Supply Co. (Samsco) were located at the corner of South Chaparral and Cooper's Alley. That long, narrow building still stands.

Doc McGregor/Corpus Christi Central Library

Ocean Drive, 1937

The "S" curve on Ocean Drive originated when a streetcar line ran from downtown to the old Alta Vista Hotel. As the road that would become Ocean Drive developed, it curved around the big resort hotel, which burned in 1927. The V.M. Donigan home (later McKinnon) on the left was built on the site of the old hotel. Plans to straighten the hairpin curves led to a hot S-Curve controversy in the late 1950s involving the sale of land on the Donigan side of the curve. Four-lane improvements in 1969 softened the sharp curve.

Old South Texas

Doc McGregor/Corpus Christi Central Library

Peoples Street, 1938
The building in the right foreground was City Hall, with the tall Jones Building in the center, and the Nueces Hotel across the street on the left. The view extended to the end of the Pleasure Pier, in its last year of existence before construction began on the seawall and the extension of the bayfront beyond Water Street.

Old South Texas

Doc McGregor/Caller-Times Archives

Caller-Times Archives

Bayfront, 1936
Before the seawall was built, extending the city two blocks into the bay, the Princess Louise Hotel on Water Street was a bayside resort hotel. The hotel opened in 1929; it was converted into an apartment complex in 1965.

Water Street, 1948
Walter Foster, proprietor (with his wife Louise) of the Princess Louise Hotel, strongly opposed building the seawall, which, he said, would cost the city millions of dollars for no good purpose. One reason for his opposition was the fact that the seawall would displace the hotel's location on the waterfront. The Princess Louise's slogan was "At The Water's Edge." Building the seawall put the Princess well inland.

Old South Texas

South Broadway, 1939

The ornate mansion built by W.W. Jones, South Texas cattleman and owner of the Nueces Hotel, became the La Retama Public Library in 1937. It housed the library until the old City Hall building at Peoples and Mesquite was remodeled for use as a library in 1955.

South Broadway, 1939
Youngsters visited the La Retama Library in the old W.W. Jones mansion on a warm summer day.

Corpus Christi, c. 1930

W.W. Jones, born in Goliad in 1858, became a cowboy at a young age, taking herds on the trail to Kansas. He built a ranching empire of 260,000 acres in three South Texas counties, with his main headquarters at his Alta Vista Ranch, 22 miles from Hebbronville. Jones owned the Nueces Hotel and the Jones Building in Corpus Christi. He died at the Medical-Professional Hospital on July 17, 1942.

Old South Texas

Caller-Times Archives

Port, 1931 and c. 1940s

The Port of Corpus Christi in 1931 (above) was limited to the main turning basin. West of the small harbor was a vast expanse of salt flats. In the middle of the Depression, port officials borrowed $400,000 to dig the Industrial Channel to Avery Point. This brought the first big port-area industry to Corpus Christi — Southern Alkali (Pittsburgh Plate Glass). Dredging the Industrial Canal and the Avery Point turning basin (right) were the first major expansion projects of the port.

Caller-Times Archives

78

Bayfront, 1937
Looking north, traffic was backed up on North Beach waiting for the bascule bridge to be lowered back into place. The counter-weight bridge (bascule means see-saw in French) was a bottleneck for traffic for more than 30 years.

Bayfront, c. 1941
The bascule bridge served as the main span across the ship channel from 1926, when the new port was opened, until Harbor Bridge replaced it in 1959. In June 1961, the old bascule bridge was removed and sold for junk.

Old South Texas

Doc McGregor/Corpus Christi Central Library

North Beach, 1939

A wall advertised the abilities of Madame Karma, "eminent astrologer." Entertainment choices on North Beach varied from dance halls, nightly musical programs, bingo, carnival rides, and sideshows like Madame Karma's.

Paul J. Madden/Corpus Christi Central Library

North Beach, 1941

Sleeping off the excesses of the night before at the rear of a bar on North Beach.

Old South Texas

Port, c. 1939

A German ship docked at the Port of Corpus Christi to take on a cargo of lead ingots from Mexico. The port was a busy place in 1939 as war loomed in Europe. When war began in 1941, domestic shipping came to a halt. The port was placed under strict security. Camouflaged ships became a commonplace; some light-colored ships were painted gray, making them more difficult to spot at sea. Some were mounted with 3-inch and 5-inch guns as protection against the U-boat menace. Commercial shipping resumed in late 1945 after ships were released by the War Shipping Administration.

Alice, 1940

A bale of cotton decorated the front of the Alice Bank & Trust, at the corner of Main and Wright, next door to the Eagle Pharmacy.

Up River Road, c. 1951

James Clark's produce market was located at the intersection of Up River Road and Navigation.

Old South Texas

S. Water, 1939
George Zackie's Play House restaurant, with curb service, was a popular place on this September day. The sign said that the special that week was a fried chicken basket for 35 cents.

Doc McGregor/Corpus Christi Central Library

Doc McGregor/Corpus Christi Central Library

Bayfront, 1939

Early in 1939, work began on the bayfront improvement project which was to completely alter the city's waterfront appearance. Dredged fill extended the city at some points to more than 1,000 feet into the bay. A 12,000-foot-long seawall was built from the port to Craig Street in the south. The seawall, the two T-Heads, and the L-Head were completed two years later, at a cost of $2.2 million.

Doc McGregor Collection/Corpus Christi Museum of Science and History

Bayfront, 1940

Dredged fill from the bay bottom increased the city's shore into the bay by roughly two blocks. The street behind the newly filled area was high-and-dry Water Street. At bottom right was what would become the barge dock.

Bayfront, 1940
Cars parked on the newly completed barge dock at the north end of the seawall.

Bayfront, 1941
The $2 million seawall, built by contractor J. DePuy of San Antonio, was finished in March 1941. The project raised the bayfront to 14 feet above sea level, or 3.4 feet above the high-water mark of the 1919 storm. This not only gave the city much greater hurricane protection, but also greater beauty.

Old South Texas

South Staples, 1940
Curb hops at the popular drive-in High Hat prided themselves on fast service. The High Hat was operated by Mrs. Aline Beaty.

Doc McGregor/Corpus Christi Museum of Science and History

Chaparral Street, 1940
Winerich Motors showed off the new model Studebaker for 1941. World War II would halt the production of passenger cars. New models were not produced until after the war.

Red Moores/Caller-Times Archives

S. Carancahua, 1954
Fire department trucks were lined up in front of the Central Fire Station. The city's first (volunteer) fire department was founded in 1871. In the early days, manpower pulled the hose carts and pumped the water to put out fires. The department gained motor-driven fire trucks in 1913.

Old South Texas

Corpus Christi Central Library

Naval Air Station, 1941
Base security personnel checked cars entering the Naval Air Station for dedication ceremonies on March 12. After war came in December, the base quickly grew in size. What began as a $43 million installation became a $125 million installation — the largest Navy air training center in the country. When the base was dedicated, it was only 70 percent completed. A visitor in early 1942 said it was nothing but sand, hangars and cement. During the war, the base payroll added $60 million a year to the Corpus Christi economy.

Naval Air Station, 1941

Secretary of the Navy Frank Knox, the former publisher of the *Chicago Daily News*, dedicated the new Navy air training base on March 12. In his speech, Knox dedicated the base to peace, but he warned that it would have to be "the peace of justice and righteousness — any other type of peace is but a mockery." On the right is the commanding officer of the base, Capt. Alva D. Bernhard, who had recently been in command of the USS Lexington. The base would play a major role in the training of Navy aviators for World War II.

Naval Air Station, 1941

The first cadets at the new Naval Air Station stand for inspection.

Old South Texas

Peoples Street, 1941

Men in front of the Nueces Hotel were reading a *Caller-Times* Extra reporting the attack on Pearl Harbor by Japan early that morning. Phones at the *Caller-Times* rang continuously that Dec. 7 Sunday as people tried to find out more about the attack. At the new Naval Air Station, all leaves were cancelled.

Caller-Times Archives

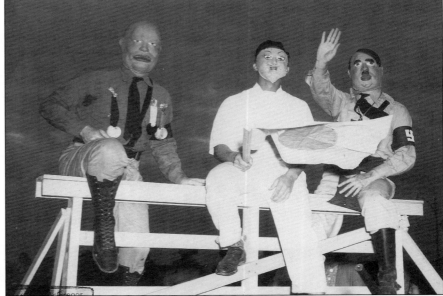

Corpus Christi Central Library

Bayfront, 1941

A defense bond parade on Dec. 20 ended with the burning in effigy of the three leaders of the Axis powers — Mussolini, Tojo and Hitler.

Caller-Times Archives

Peoples Street, 1942

A blackout warden made his rounds on Peoples Street, stopping to check for a light in the window of Daly's Camera Store. U-boat sightings in the Gulf led to blackouts along the Texas coast during World War II. Oil tankers and other transport ships would be easy targets when silhouetted against city lights.

Caller-Times Archives

Naval Air Station, 1942
During World War II, all photographs taken at the Naval Air Station were censored. This shot of enlisted sailors was not allowed to be published without cropping to keep the size of the training program secret. On the back of the negative was written: "CENSOR. Will not permit use this part."

Chaparral, 1942
Two months after the attack on Pearl Harbor, Centre Theatre joined the war effort with its marquee pushing war bonds. A "Victory Booth" was manned in the lobby to sell war bonds and stamps.

Aransas Pass, 1941
Sailors outside a fishing guide establishment. During the war, island beaches were off-limits and fishing outside the jetties was prohibited. Because of the threat from German U-boats, embedded gun emplacements on Mustang Island guarded the Aransas Pass channel.

Doc McGregor/Corpus Christi Central Library

North Beach, 1942
A sailor and girlfriend on North Beach. In the 1940s, North Beach attracted 4,000 visitors a day on a weekend, 20,000 on a holiday.

Corpus Christi, 1942
A Home Guard unit drilled in a warehouse in the port area.

Paul Madden/Corpus Christi Central Library

Leopard Street, 1941
Saturday on Leopard Street in 1941. Beyond the Jalisco Restaurant, owned by Roy Pizzini, was the Grande Café and the Grande Theater. Further down the street was the Jalisco Tortilla Shop, also owned by Pizzini. Most of the prominent Hispanic-owned businesses were concentrated on or near Leopard Street in the 1930s and '40s. These included the Mirabal Print Shop, Galvan Pharmacy, Pena's Meat Market, and others.

Cabaniss Field, 1946

Cadets check the flight schedule board at Cabaniss Field. The end of World War II on Sept. 2, 1945, ushered in a period of uncertainty about the future of the Corpus Christi Naval Air Station and its outlying fields. Waldron, Rodd and Cuddihy fields were all closed in late 1946 and early 1947. Cabaniss remained in operation until January 1948, when it was decommissioned. The field was reopened later that year as a separate command, and it stayed in operation until 1958.

Caller-Times Archives

Naval Air Station, 1944

Three SNJs fly in echelon above the clouds over Naval Air Station Corpus Christi. More than 35,000 naval aviators were trained at Corpus Christi NAS and its outlying fields of Rodd, Cabaniss, Cuddihy and Waldron during World War II.

U.S. Navy Photo/Caller-Times Archives

Old South Texas

Mesquite Street, 1941
Shuffleboard players in Artesian Park.

Paul Madden/Corpus Christi Central Library

Doc McGregor/Corpus Christi Museum of Science and History

Water Street, 1942
Women work as service station attendants at the Texas Star No. 3, across from the Nueces Hotel. During the war, women all over the country took employment that had been exclusively thought of as jobs for men.

Sam Rankin St., 1942
Tomas Cantu and family operated Cantu's Food Store at 807 Sam Rankin St.

Old South Texas

South Staples, 1941
At the Holly Beauty Salon were (from left) Ruby McMillan, Frances Tradalier, Dot Vetters, shop owner Irene Holly (standing), manicurist Nina Huggins (sitting, right). The woman behind her was unidentified. Hair dryers of that time heated air with natural gas, with electric motors used to blow the hot air into the hoods.

Caller-Times Archives

Old South Texas

Doc McGregor/Katherine Hrissikopoulos

Chaparral Street, 1943
Charlie K. Hrissikopoulos (pronounced kris-cop-olous), owner of the Olympia Confectionery, oversees the preparation of boxes of candy mailed to U.S. troops overseas. The Olympia, at the corner of the Nueces Hotel, was, as the *Caller's* Bob McCracken once described it, "the hub of the local universe" for Corpus Christi teenagers for more than three decades. Hrissikopoulos opened the confectionery in 1919; he sold the business in 1955.

Caller-Times Archives

Brownsville Road, c. 1940s
George Herman "Babe" Ruth at Cliff Maus Field on a visit to Corpus Christi. Ruth died in 1948.

North Beach, 1942
The saltwater pool, with water piped in from the bay, was a favorite swimming place. The pool, built in the 1920s by Bruce Collins, was part of the bathhouse complex at the beach. It was demolished in the 1950s for the construction of the Sandy Shores Hotel

Calallen, c. 1945
New Noakes, the longtime postmaster at Calallen, was the son of Thomas J. Noakes, storekeeper at old Nuecestown. New was a little over a year old when bandits from below the Rio Grande raided the town in 1875 and burned his father's store. New as a baby was carried by his older brother and sister to escape the bandits. New got his name because he was born on New Year's Day, 1873. He died in 1957.

North Beach, 1941
Riding the ferris wheel on North Beach. North Beach's development as an entertainment center took off after the 1919 storm when a bathhouse, saltwater pool, dance hall and carnival midway were opened.

Old South Texas

Chaparral Street, 1946

Some 10,000 people turned out on June 18, 1946, for a parade for Admiral Chester W. Nimitz, a native of Fredericksburg who commanded U.S. forces in the Pacific. Nimitz in his speech said that Corpus Christi would always play an important role for the Navy. The Nimitz Day Parade was considered the city's largest since the Port Opening Day parade in 1926.

Carl Graf/Caller-Times Archives

Old South Texas

Caller-Times Archives

Chaparral, 1945
After Japan's surrender on Sept. 2, bringing World War II to an end, the streets of Corpus Christi were decorated for Christmas for the first time in four years.

Old South Texas

Doc McGregor/Caller-Times Archives

North Mesquite, c. 1940s
Former world heavyweight boxing champion Jack Dempsey was in Corpus Christi to referee a wrestling match at the Town Hall Arena. Someone in the crowd yelled to ask Dempsey if he was man enough to go a few rounds and Dempsey stripped off his shirt and invited anyone in the audience to take him on.

Courtesy of David C. Morrow

Shoreline Boulevard, c. 1946
A giant jackrabbit served as a photographer's set-up pose on Shoreline.

King Ranch, 1949

Hollywood star Roy Rogers, "the King of Cowboys," with the children of Richard M. Kleberg Jr. during a visit to King Ranch.

Ocean Drive, 1949

The late Jack Maddux owned and operated Oso Pier and Bait Stand. Maddux once said of his business, "If you don't like fishing and talking about fishing, this could get to be like work."

Old South Texas

Shoreline Boulevard, 1948
Candidate Lyndon B. Johnson, with a wide grin, rushed under the helicopter rotors to shake hands with the waiting crowd in a field on the bayfront (where Memorial Coliseum was later built) in the Senate campaign of 1948.

Caller-Times Archives

Box 13

The runoff election for the U.S. Senate in 1948 between Lyndon Johnson and former Texas Gov. Coke Stevenson was a fierce battle that became the closest senatorial contest in American history. For five days after the election, Stevenson thought he had won. Out of nearly one million votes cast, he had a 112-vote lead. Then, on the sixth day, Precinct 13 in Alice, in Jim Wells County, reported an amended return. There were 203 additional votes, 201 of them for Johnson, enough to give him the election with a margin of 87 votes. The amended return was immediately challenged. Stevenson himself showed up at a bank in Alice where the returns were kept, and looked over the tally sheets for Box 13. He found that the last 203 names were added in alphabetical order, and all were written in the same blue ink.

When the case was taken to court in Jim Wells County, and Box 13 opened in court, the tally sheets Stevenson had seen were missing. Johnson was certified as the winner, while an angry Stevenson said, "I was beaten by a stuffed ballot box." Box 13 gave Johnson the election, the mocking nickname of "Landslide Lyndon," and changed the course of American history.

Old South Texas

Alice, 1948
Former Gov. Coke Stevenson (right) outside a courtroom in Alice.

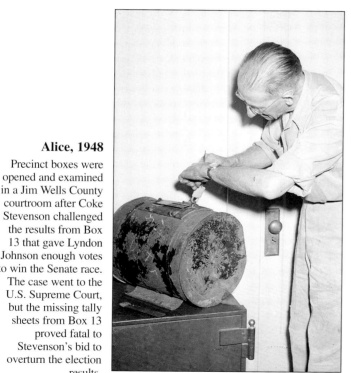

Alice, 1948
Precinct boxes were opened and examined in a Jim Wells County courtroom after Coke Stevenson challenged the results from Box 13 that gave Lyndon Johnson enough votes to win the Senate race. The case went to the U.S. Supreme Court, but the missing tally sheets from Box 13 proved fatal to Stevenson's bid to overturn the election results.

Alice, 1948
Precinct 13 in Alice reported an amended return that added 201 votes for Lyndon B. Johnson, giving him a victory over Coke Stevenson in the closest Senate election in Texas history. It was always assumed, but never proved, that Johnson called George B. Parr, a political power in South Texas, and told him how many votes he would need to win, and that Parr ordered the Box 13 fix. Shown with Box 13 were (left to right) Stokes Misenhimer, Alice police chief; Hubert Sain, Jim Wells County sheriff; Givens Parr, brother of George Parr and a vice president of the Parr-controlled bank in Alice where election precinct boxes were stored; E.G. Lloyd and Barney Goldthorn.

Old South Texas

Upper Broadway, 1939
The McKenzie Construction Co. prepared the site for the foundation of the Robert Driscoll Hotel, which was built next door to the White Plaza Hotel on the bluff.

Upper Broadway, 1949
Towering over its neighbors on the bluff, the Driscoll Hotel in the 1940s was the city's tallest building. A court dispute between the White Plaza Hotel and Clara and her brother Robert Driscoll was often cited as the main reason for Clara Driscoll having the new hotel built. She named it after her brother Robert, who died in 1929.

Old South Texas

Doc McGregor/Corpus Christi Central Library

Some members of the 1950 Miller graduating class "make a leg" while posing for class pictures. They were (left to right) Wanda Hull, Frances Zoch, Sharie Willingham, Barbara Airheart, Becky Scott, Janet Howard, Juana Lee Kuenstler, Virginia Warren and Nancy Cairns.

Old South Texas

North Miami, c. 1950
Corpus Christi oilman Sam E. Wilson and his wife Ada were on vacation in Miami at the Golden Strand Hotel. Wherever she went, Ada Wilson would make sure that publicity photos were sent back to the *Caller-Times*. She was the founder of the Ada Wilson Hospital for Crippled Children.

Bayfront, 1950
Part of Sydney Herndon's fleet of shrimp boats anchored at the L-Head in Corpus Christi Bay. Herndon moved his fishing fleet and wholesale fish business to Aransas Pass in 1956 in a dispute with the city of Corpus Christi over marina rental fees.

Old South Texas

Red Moores/Caller-Times Archives

Red Moores/Caller-Times Archives

N. Broadway, 1950

ABOVE: Members of Company B, 15th Marine Infantry, composed of 80 young men from Corpus Christi and surrounding area, departed from the Missouri Pacific depot for training in California in preparation for the Korean War. Hundreds of relatives and friends gathered at the train depot to see the unit off. Some of these men ended up with the 7th Marines in the desperate fighting around the Chosin Reservoir of North Korea.

RIGHT: A young woman kissed her Marine boyfriend goodbye as the members of Company B, 15th Marine Infantry, left on Aug. 6 for training for the Korean War.

King Ranch, 1953
During a roundup in a dust storm, King Ranch manager Robert J. Kleberg Jr. cut out calves from a herd of Santa Gertrudis cattle.

Old South Texas

King Ranch, c. 1920
Family and friends on the steps of the Big House at King Ranch. Some of them were Robert Kleberg Sr., (bottom center); former Corpus Christi Mayor Roy Miller (bottom left); Henrietta King, widow of Richard King (in chair at top); Alice Kleberg East holding her son Tom East (center); and Maud (Heaney) Miller, Roy Miller's wife (upper right).

Murphy Givens Collection

The King Ranch

Richard King, a 30-year-old steamboat captain on the Rio Grande, bought a spread of grassy prairie on Santa Gertrudis Creek in 1853. It was a remote area between Corpus Christi and Brownsville. King paid $300 for 15,000 acres — about two cents an acre.

King and his partner "Legs" Lewis stocked the ranch with longhorns bought in Mexico. King convinced *vaqueros* and their families to move up from a small Mexican village to live on his ranch and work his cattle. They became "*Los Kinenos*" — King People.

During the Civil War, King organized the Cotton Road, which became a lifeline for the Confederacy. King and Mifflin Kenedy became wealthy carrying and selling cotton for the Confederacy. After the war, King began enlarging his ranch. When he died of stomach cancer at age 60, he had increased the original holding of 15,000 acres to more than 500,000 acres. It was one of the largest cattle ranches in the world, and would continue to expand to almost one million acres. Richard King's widow Henrietta survived him by 40 years; she died at age 92 on the ranch where she had lived for 70 years.

Doc McGregor/Caller-Times Archives

King Ranch, c. 1940

The front entrance of the 25-room Santa Gertrudis ranch home — "the Big House." The ranch house was built in 1912 by Robert J. Kleberg Sr. at a cost of $350,000. It was patterned after a hacienda Kleberg had seen in Mexico.

Caller-Times Archives

King Ranch, 1991

The "Big House" at King Ranch 50 years later.

Caller-Times Archives

Jim Wells, c. 1900

Jim Wells, born on St. Joseph's Island in 1850, became the undisputed Democratic political boss in Brownsville. As Richard King's lawyer, he played an important role in the history of the King Ranch. Judge Wells died in 1923; Jim Wells County was named for him.

Old South Texas

King Ranch, c.1950
A King Ranch hand used a lead steer at roundup time. In working cattle not used to pens and corrals, the presence of a lead steer helps soothe nervous cattle.

Caller-Times Archives

Rockport, 1955
When it was dedicated in 1940, Rockport's new yacht basin gained the nickname of "the fish bowl" for its shape. Building the basin demolished part of the rocky point that gave Rockport its name.

Caller-Times Archives

Bayfront, 1959
Dr. William Frederick "Doc" McGregor, a chiropractor, took most of the photographs that appeared in the *Caller-Times* in the 1930s and early 1940s. He was the paper's official photographer, but he wasn't paid a salary. All he wanted, he once told the editor, was the credit line — "Photo by McGregor." He took many thousands of photos of Corpus Christi and the area for more than 30 years. He was severely beaten by a burglar in 1977; he died in 1986.

Caller-Times Archives

Corpus Christi, 1957
J. Frank Dobie, a master storyteller, published "The Vaquero of the Brush Country" in 1929. Other books followed, including "The Mustangs," "The Longhorns," "Coronado's Children." He wrote about his memories of growing up on a ranch in Live Oak County for the *Caller-Times* in 1959. He wrote "my horse Buck pointing his ears when I walked into the pen to rope out a mount and seeming to ask if I were going to ride him or Brownie . . . the green of mesquites in the early spring . . . the stillness of the night broken by windmill lifting rods . . . the rhythm of a saddle's squeak in the night . . . these the land gave me."

Caller-Times Archives

Rockport, 1957

The Aransas County Courthouse, built in 1890, was designed by one of the country's most famous architects, J. Riley Gordon. Although it was considered an architectural treasure, this unusual and handsome mosque-style courthouse was torn down in 1956.

Old South Texas

Shoreline Boulevard, 1961
Vice President Lyndon Johnson, Lady Bird Johnson, and Corpus Christi Mayor Ben McDonald (back seat) led a delegation from Washington that visited Padre Island before Padre Island National Seashore was established.

LBJ Ranch, 1960
South Texans visited Sen. Lyndon B. Johnson, soon to become Vice President Johnson. Left to right were Dr. Hector P. Garcia, Johnson, Dr. Clotilde Garcia, Mrs. and Mr. Reynaldo Garza.

Corpus Christi Central Library

Nueces River, c. 1950
The Lagarto Bridge spanned the Nueces River until the new Wesley Seale Dam was built in 1958. The bridge was cut from its supports and dropped into the channel of the river in 1959. The old bridge is at the bottom of Lake Corpus Christi.

Caller-Times Archives

Lake Corpus Christi, 1959
When the new Wesley Seale Dam was built, the steel in the floodgates of the old La Fruta Dam (sometimes called the Old Mathis Dam) was supposed to be salvaged, but each gate disappeared under the surface of the lake and the salvage company could not drag them to the shore. The area where the old gates went down was made a restricted area.

Gulf, 1958
Oilman Gus Glasscock's first oil platform in the Gulf — Mr. Gus I, built in 1949 — capsized in heavy seas in 1957 and had to be salvaged. That same year, Glasscock had Mr. Gus II built.

Wilson Building, 1960
C.G. (Gus) Glasscock, a pioneer Corpus Christi oilman, was considered crazy when he decided in 1949 to build a huge mobile floating barge from which to drill oil wells in the tidelands of the Gulf. But Glasscock helped revolutionize the search for oil in deep waters. He bought a site on the bayfront off Ocean Drive, filled it, and had dreams of building a luxury hotel there. He later sold the Glasscock Fill site.

Old South Texas

Caller-Times Archives

Naval Air Station, 1959
On the afternoon of June 30, Ray H. Bostick, assistant personnel director, was the last man to lock up and leave the Navy's Overhaul & Repair facility. Since the beginning of World War II, the Navy's O&R at Corpus Christi had overhauled, converted and repaired Navy aircraft, engines, and manufactured parts, tools and equipment.

Caller-Times Archives

Naval Air Station, 1959
On a cold, gloomy day in February, laid-off workers at the Navy's Overhaul & Repair facility at the Corpus Christi Naval Air Station moved through a check-out line in an unheated hangar. This was the first batch of more than 3,000 civil service employees who were laid off in stages. The Navy employed civilian workers to overhaul and repair aircraft and engines. The shutdown was announced before Christmas 1958. Closing the O&R was a severe blow to the Corpus Christi economy.

Old South Texas

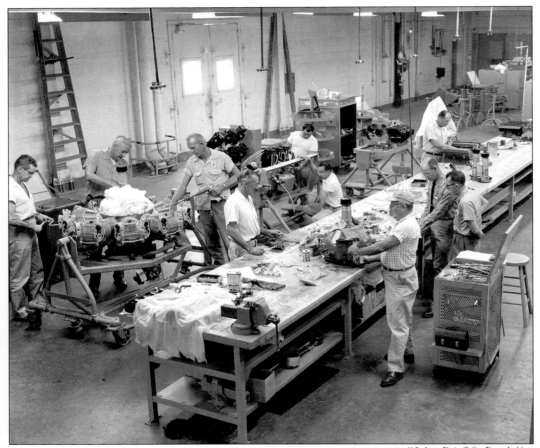

U.S. Army Photo/Caller-Times Archives

Naval Air Station, 1961

Workers in the engine assembly shop at the new Army Maintenance Center (now the Army Depot) were (left to right): B.H. Rainey, Ludy Benjamin, E.M. Hunt, L. Wyman, B. Gonzales, C.A. Garza, C.S. Garcia, Harold Moore, O.F. Swinnea and W.E. McMahon.

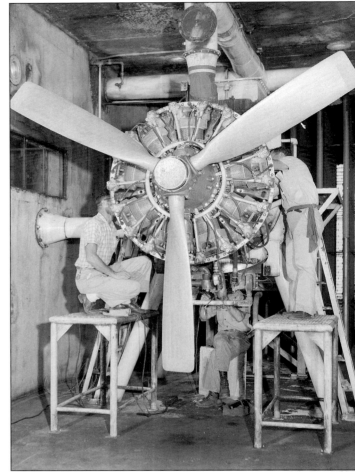

Caller-Times Archives

Naval Air Station, 1961

On June 22, workers at the new Army Maintenance Center began the process of prototyping a Wright engine. The process called for taking the engine apart, overhauling, reassembling and testing it. The various parts and operations were photographed as training aids. This operation was designed to set the pattern for regular engine overhaul and repair work.

Old South Texas

Aransas Pass, c. 1957
The one-way, rickety Port Aransas Causeway linked Aransas Pass to Harbor Island and the ferry landing to Port A. It was built as a railroad trestle in 1926. A track-mounted truck pulled a string of railroad cars on which cars were loaded. It was paved over in 1931 and used until a new highway department causeway was built in 1961.

c. 1930

Cliff Maus was Corpus Christi's first airport manager. He left Corpus Christi in 1932 to fly for Braniff; he was killed in a plane crash in Fort Worth three years later. The municipal airport was renamed the Cliff Maus Field in his memory.

Old Brownsville Road, 1949

Cliff Maus Field, Corpus Christi's municipal airport, featured regular flights by Braniff, Eastern and Trans Texas Airways. The field was built in 1928 on a 180-acre tract. The city became interested in air travel after Charles Lindbergh flew over Corpus Christi on a flight to Mexico after his historic flight over the Atlantic. The new airport was later named for World War I ace William Clifford Maus, the airport's first manager.

Old South Texas

Old Brownsville Road, 1960

The tower at the old Cliff Maus Field cast a long shadow as dignitaries — including Mayor Ellroy King and Eastern Airlines President Eddie Rickenbacker — prepared to board a plane for a short flight to the new Corpus Christi International Airport on Aug. 6, 1960. In 1955, the city chose a site for a new airport east of Clarkwood. The final cost for building the new facility was $6 million.

Old South Texas

Caller-Times Archives

West Broadway, 1962
Corpus Christi's last passenger train left the Missouri-Pacific Depot at 10:05 a.m. on June 30, marking the end of a long era of daily passenger train service that began in 1880 when Uriah Lott's Corpus Christi, San Diego and Rio Grande Railroad (later the Tex-Mex) began rail service. That was followed by the San Antonio and Aransas Pass Railway, which reached Corpus Christi in 1886 after building a trestle bridge across Nueces Bay. Then came the St. Louis, Brownsville and Mexico Railroad, which began operations in 1904.

Old South Texas

Corpus Christi Central Library

Caller-Times Archives

Corpus Christi, 1962
Fred Gipson, author of "Old Yeller," which became a hit Disney movie, returned to visit the *Caller-Times* where he had worked in the 1930s. Longtime editor Bob McCracken once sent Gipson, in his scuffed cowboy boots, to write a story about a ballet recital. After the review came out, the dance teacher came to see McCracken to complain about "that awful cowboy" and McCracken wrote that she didn't leave until she had lost her voice.

Corpus Christi, 1965
Striking longshoremen played dominoes in front of a blackboard with picket duty assignments. The nationwide strike ended on Feb. 28 after 49 days. The strike stranded a number of ships in the Port of Corpus Christi.

Old South Texas

Lower Broadway, 1960
Victor Hugo Herold, longtime city editor of the *Corpus Christi Times*, was known as a creature of habit. He wore the same type clothes and he never took off his windbreaker in the office. Each Tuesday, after the *Times*' edition was put to bed, he always took a one-hour nap in the photo lab. This was Tuesday.

Lower Broadway, 1936
The new *Caller-Times*' building was completed in October 1935. The paper's offices had been at 405 Mesquite since the 1920s. The move began on Saturday night, after the Sunday edition was printed. The move was finished in time to print Monday's edition.

Ocean Drive, 2000
Edward H. Harte, former publisher of the *Caller-Times*, donated $46 million to Texas A&M University-Corpus Christi to establish a research center, later named the Harte Research Institute for Gulf of Mexico Studies. It was one of the largest gifts ever received by a Texas university.

Lower Broadway, 1967
After Edward H. Harte was named publisher of the *Caller-Times* in 1962, he said he always knew he would get the job of the family-owned Harte-Hanks' paper "if I behaved myself." He worked as reporter and editor at San Angelo before his promotion. He retired in 1987. Harte-Hanks sold its newspapers to the E.W. Scripps Co. in 1997.

Old South Texas

Corpus Christi, 1966

Brother Leo (Roderick Norton "Christopher" Gregory), a former Trappist monk, signed his name on June 28, 1966, to 1.2 million words taken in deposition in the contested will of Sarita Kenedy East, granddaughter of cattle baron Mifflin Kenedy. Before she died in 1961, she named Brother Leo as the sole executor of her estate, then valued at $500 million. Brother Leo eventually lost control of the Kenedy Foundation funds.

Caller-Times Archives

When Sarita Kenedy East died in 1961, she left an estate valued at more than $500 million to the care of a former Trappist monk, Brother Leo.

Port at Tarlton, 1965

It was a rainy day in February in front of the Buccaneer Drive-In.

Corpus Christi Central Library

Old South Texas

Caller-Times Archives

Ocean Drive, 1961
Resident students arriving at the University of Corpus Christi were forced to take a boat ride to get to the campus after Hurricane Carla washed out the Oso Bridge at Ocean Drive. The rope-powered ferry was the only way to get to Ward Island until Army Engineers brought in a portable bridge.

Ocean Drive, 1961
Hurricane Carla took a bite out of Ocean Drive, near Montclair, when waves generated by the storm eroded the ground underneath.

Caller-Times Archives

Port Lavaca, 1961
Bent road sign pole actually showed the direction of Hurricane Carla.

Caller-Times Archives

Old South Texas

Sinton, 1967
Hurricane Beulah brought more than 30 inches of rain that flooded one-half million acres of South Texas, including always flood-prone Sinton.

Old South Texas

Padre Island, c. 1950

Pat Dunn's ranch house and corral on Padre Island. After the 1916 hurricane destroyed his two-story home near Packery Channel, Dunn built a new ranch house at the head of the island. Dunn, who ran cattle on Padre Island for 50 years, had an unusual ranch. No fences were needed — cowboys herded cattle from the southern tip of the island to holding pens up the island. During Dunn's lifetime, about 4,000 head of cattle were pastured on the island. Many were killed in the 1916, '19, and '33 storms. After Padre Island was dedicated as a National Seashore, in 1967, cattle continued grazing on the island for three more years, until Dec. 31, 1970.

Caller-Times Archives

Old South Texas

Padre Island, 1968
Lady Bird Johnson, the first lady, spoke at the dedication of the Padre Island National Seashore on April 9. The podium was built of island driftwood.

Caller-Times Archives

North Beach, 1937
Aerial shot of North Beach (when it was still officially North Beach), with the famous Breakers Hotel in the center.

North Beach, 1948
The Breakers Hotel was built in 1912 as the Corpus Christi Beach Hotel. It was converted to a U.S. Army convalescent hospital for wounded World War I soldiers. The building, still in use as a hospital, was one of the few structures to withstand the 1919 hurricane. The upper floors became a refuge for storm victims. The hurricane smashed the walls on the first floor, but the reinforced concrete framework of the building prevented its collapse. It survived that storm, but fell to another one five decades later.

Caller-Times Archives

Bayfront, 1970
Storm flags fly at the Corpus Christi Marina Office on the Lawrence St. T-Head as Hurricane Celia comes ashore. What had been predicted as a mild storm strengthened before it hit. An article described Celia's unpredictability: "It was such an ordinary August day . . . then Celia came — small, sneaky, lopsided and unconventional, behaving as no hurricane ever had. For four fearful hours, she clawed her way across the Coastal Bend" — the worst disaster since the 1919 hurricane.

Old South Texas

Aransas Pass, 1970
Hurricane Celia slammed dozens of shrimp boats against the north end of Conn Brown Harbor, home port for the Gulf shrimping fleet. Some shrimp boats were blown ashore, some piled on top of others, and some sank. Many of the wooden hulled boats were sunk in or near the harbor.

Aransas Pass, 1970
Salvage work began on a wrecked shrimp boat at Conn Brown Harbor. At the harbor, the newer steel-hulled vessels suffered only minor damage while many wooden-hulled boats were sunk in the harbor or severely damaged. The storm's reported tides were: 12 feet at Conn Brown Harbor, 5 feet at Rockport, 5 feet at Mustang Island, and minus 4.5 feet at Corpus Christi marina.

Old South Texas

A Storm Named Celia

Caller-Times Archives

Aransas Pass, 1970
Sitting in the storm wreckage in the Conn Brown Harbor area in the aftermath of Celia. Scores of shrimp boats were damaged or destroyed in the storm, which was supposed to be no big deal, "something like a strong norther."

On Sunday, Aug. 2, 1970, Celia was predicted to hit the upper Gulf Coast with winds of 90 miles an hour. It was described as a benign storm, "more show than blow." On Sunday night, it gained intensity and changed direction, aiming at the Corpus Christi area.

On Monday, the eye of the storm moved just north of Corpus Christi at 3:45 p.m. Wind velocity hit 140 miles per hour at Ingleside and 118 mph at Corpus Christi, with gusts reaching 161 mph for 30-second intervals. Windows in downtown buildings were shattered, trees uprooted, roofs, porches, shutters and fences blown away. Tree limbs were scattered like straw. Boats were beached, and cars and trucks were overturned on city streets.

The storm left Corpus Christi without power and telephone service. Rescue efforts that night were hampered by lack of communications. In the few areas where power was still on, alarms sounded ominously. Policemen armed with rifles stood guard to prevent looting. One man returned to his demolished apartment to find that the only thing standing was a small table on which the phone sat, and it was still working.

Ice was a precious commodity throughout the city. When one man died, his friends took ice to the grieving family instead of flowers.

Celia had unusual features. Corpus Christi was on the storm's left, typically a hurricane's weak side, but that was not the case with Celia. It was not a "wet" storm, or the damage would have been greater. Celia caused tides in Corpus Christi Bay to drop, rather than rise. Boats moored in the marina ended up sitting on the bottom of the bay until the tide came back in.

It was miraculous that only four people in Corpus Christi died as a result of the storm, although the damage in Nueces County amounted to $335 million. For years, people would begin a sentence with, "Before Celia" or "After Celia." It was the city's worst hurricane since the deadly storm of 1919.

Chaparral, 1970

In Celia's wake, a car was demolished and partly covered with bricks in front of the Alamo Pawnshop at Chaparral and Starr streets.

Old South Texas

Caller-Times Archives

Staples at Doddridge, 1970
Hurricane Celia struck on Monday, Aug. 3, 1970, leaving widespread devastation behind its wake. By the following day, the National Guard was on duty to enforce a curfew, prevent looting, and man centers for the distribution of food, such as this one located at the Corpus Christi Fire Department station on Staples.

Old South Texas

George Tuley/Caller-Times Archives

Nueces Bay Causeway, 1970
Looking south, toward Corpus Christi. During Hurricane Celia, Capt. Clark's Showboat, with 11 people on board, broke away from its moorings in the city marina. The boat was blown out in the bay and then back to the causeway area. Celia played games with the bay; instead of rising, the tide dropped four and a half feet, damaging the hulls of many boats.

Old South Texas

Lexington Boulevard, 1970
A man surveyed the wreckage of the Gateway Mobile Home Park after Hurricane Celia struck.

George Tuley/Caller-Times Archives

Old South Texas

Corpus Christi, 1959

George B. Parr walked out of the federal courthouse on Starr Street in Corpus Christi in June 1959. Parr and seven others were convicted of defrauding the Benavides school district by cashing checks made out to fictitious persons. Parr, the "Duke of Duval," was also called "*jefe*" and "*patron grande*" by his followers in Duval County.

Caller-Times Archives

The Parr Dynasty

The Parr dynasty dates to 1883, when Archie Parr was hired as foreman of the Sweden Ranch. He became a county commissioner and state senator, controlling patronage in a large area of South Texas. When he retired, he turned over his empire to son George B. Parr, who ruled Duval as a fiefdom. Parr was suspected of orchestrating the Box 13 fraud in Jim Wells County that gave the 1948 Senate election to Lyndon Johnson. Beginning in the '50s, state investigators found a wide trail of graft and corruption. Parr's downfall began with an IRS investigation that led to his conviction in 1974. On April 1, 1975, after he failed to appear in court, his body was found on the family ranch near Benavides; he had been shot in the head.

Parr's nephew Archer was found guilty of lying to a grand jury. Judge D.W. Suttle's words at the sentencing could be taken to apply to the Parr dynasty as a whole: "The record in this case tells the story of the power of the defendant Archer Parr in Duval County; that such power is virtually absolute; that such absolute power has corrupted him absolutely. That the exercise of such power by the defendant Archer Parr has prostituted the democratic and judicial process in Duval County, and constitutes a threat and danger to law and order, to the citizens, taxpayers, and public and private properties located in Duval County, Texas."

San Diego, 1950

George B. Parr (center) at a meeting with fellow Duval County commissioners at the Duval County Courthouse. Parr inherited a political dynasty from his father Archie Parr that fed on fraud and corruption and was kept in power by bribery and intimidation.

New Braunfels, 1957

Duval County political boss George B. Parr talked to his attorneys, Luther Jones of Corpus Christi and Percy Foreman of Houston, at Parr's trial in New Braunfels on charges of conspiring to steal funds from the Benavides Independent School District. He was found guilty and sentenced to 10 years in prison; the verdict was overturned on appeal.

Old South Texas

Kingsville, 1977
Archer Parr, nephew of George B. Parr and part of the corrupt political machine in Duval County, carried his belongings as he was being moved from the Kleberg County Jail to the Cameron County Jail. Parr was sentenced to prison terms totaling 30 years for lying to a federal grand jury.

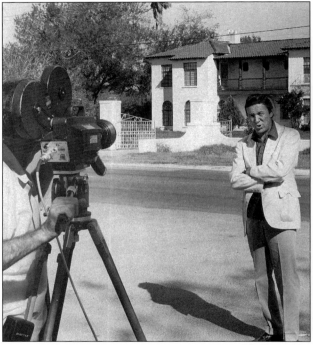

San Diego, 1975
Mike Wallace of CBS's "60 Minutes" was in San Diego in September to do a story on George B. Parr. Wallace was doing his "stand-up" in front of Parr's house.

Old South Texas

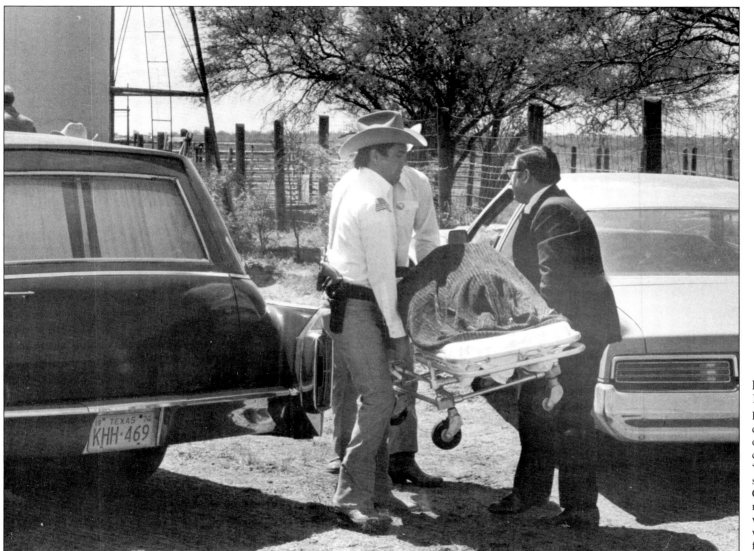

Joe Coudert/Caller-Times Archives

Los Horcones Ranch, 1975

Duval County sheriff's deputies removed the body of George B. Parr from his car on April 1, 1975. The "Duke of Duval" had been shot once in the head; his Colt .45 pistol was found nearby. Parr's car was in a wooded grove beside a windmill and pond on the family ranch at Los Horcones, near Benavides.

Mesquite Street, 1977

On July 29, Marion Uehlinger, Nueces County clerk, became the first county official to move from the 64-year-old courthouse, built in 1914, to the new $19.6 million courthouse off Leopard Street. Mrs. Uehlinger retired in 1990 after 42 years as a county employee and elected official; she died in 1995.

Cabaniss Field, 1984

Seagulls practice touch-and-go landings at the Navy's old Cabaniss Field, which was built for Navy aviator training in World War II. The base is still used for touch-and-go landings by trainees at Corpus Christi Naval Air Station.

Old South Texas

Shoreline Boulevard, 1976

Jason Luby, a maverick politician and flamboyant mayor of Corpus Christi, resigned his office to run for Congress in 1978. Luby refused to leave City Council chambers after announcing his candidacy and was removed by two uniformed policemen. He finished third in the race. He ran again for Congress in 1982, as a Republican, but lost to Solomon Ortiz.

Shoreline Boulevard, 1978

Mayor Gabe Lozano Sr. at a Corpus Christi City Council meeting. Lozano became the city's first Hispanic mayor in 1978 when he was appointed to replace Jason Luby, who resigned the mayor's office to run for Congress. Lozano had been on the council since 1959. He was known as a stabilizing leader for the city at a critical time. He died in 1984.

Ohio Street, 1980

Edmundo E. Mireles and his wife Jovita led the fight for bilingual education. Edmundo launched the teaching of Spanish in Corpus Christi elementary schools in 1940, making Corpus Christi the first in the country with such a program. He had to overcome a Texas law from 1917 that prohibited teaching a foreign language in elementary grades. He and Jovita, also a teacher, wrote textbooks used nationally on Spanish instruction.

Old South Texas

Caller-Times Archives

Ingleside-on-the-Bay

The proposed site for another Navy base in the Coastal Bend was narrowed to Ingleside Point, between the oil tanks (top) and the community of Ingleside-on-the-Bay (bottom). The Corpus Christi area was one of six finalists for a Navy homeport before the Navy decided on the Ingleside location. Original plans called for the base to host the battleship USS Wisconsin and the aircraft carrier USS Lexington. The Lexington was decommissioned in 1991 and the Wisconsin mothballed. The Navy in 1991 decided to station mine-hunting ships at Naval Station Ingleside.

Shoreline Boulevard, 1985

At a news conference at the Chamber of Commerce, Nueces County Judge Robert N. Barnes (from left), Corpus Christi Mayor Luther Jones, state Sen. Carlos Truan and state Rep. Hugo Berlanga held up early editions of the *Corpus Christi Times* announcing that Ingleside was chosen for a new Navy base.

Shoreline Boulevard, 1985

Rep. Solomon Ortiz at the Chamber of Commerce received the news on July 2 that the Corpus Christi area would gain a new Navy base at Ingleside.

Old South Texas

National Drive, 1985
Mayor Luther Jones and 3-year-old Stephanie Pollack after groundbreaking ceremonies for the Greenwood Children's Center. Jones, a former commander of the Army Depot, served four terms as mayor of Corpus Christi; he was known as a great ambassador for the city. He died in 2002.

Caller-Times Archives

1992
Mayor Luther Jones served four terms as mayor, from 1979 until 1987.

Caller-Times Archives

Old South Texas

Dave Shippee/Caller-Times Archives

Shaeffer Ranch, 1983

Cowboy Ramon Pena Resendez took off his chaps after a day's work on the Shaeffer Ranch near Orange Grove. Resendez was killed two months later in an accident while roping a calf. South Texas' earliest economy was based on cattle ranching. Walter Prescott Webb in "The Great Plains" wrote that the Nueces Valley gave birth to the cattle industry, where "men on horseback began to handle cattle on the open range instead of on foot in small pastures and cow lots."

Paul Iverson/Caller-Times Archives

Naval Station Ingleside, 1992
Tugs pushed the decommissioned USS Lexington away from the dock for its short trip across the bay for its new home off Corpus Christi Beach as the Lexington Museum on the Bay. The historic vessel was named to the National Register of Historic Places on July 31, 2003.

George Gongora/Caller-Times Archives

Cunningham Middle School, 1994

Tejano star Selena Quintanilla-Perez performed during a school visit the year before she was shot to death in Corpus Christi. Her death stunned the nation, especially the Hispanic community of her hometown. The young singer was shot to death by the founder of her fan club, Yolanda Saldivar, who was convicted of murder and sentenced to life in prison.

Tom Fox/Caller-Times Archives

Memorial Medical Center, 1995

Relatives of Selena were told that the young singer had died after she had been shot earlier that day by the founder of her fan club.

Old South Texas

Ely Hogue/Caller-Times Archives

Bayfront, 1997

Mayor Mary Rhodes, on April 12, stood inside a pipe destined for the Lake Texana pipeline. The 101-mile, $132 million project was built, over intense political opposition, largely because of her leadership and determination. The pipeline was renamed in her honor in 1998. She died of breast cancer less than two months after this photograph was taken.

Old South Texas

Doc McGregor/Corpus Christi Museum of Science and Technology

Port Aransas, 1937
The ferry boat Estelle took a load of cars from Port Aransas to Harbor Island across the ship channel. The Nellie B. joined the Estelle in 1937; the Ruby was built in 1947, and the H.C. Petry Jr. in 1960. The ferry boat service was operated by Nueces County (there was a $1 toll for a time) until the state took over responsibility in 1968. The rides are free now.

Index

A
Alice 52
Alice Bank & Trust 82
Allen, Calvin J. 5
Aransas County Courthouse 117
Aransas (Del Mar) Hotel 18
Aransas Pass land sale 28-29
Army Depot 122
Artesian Park, 15, 97

B
Bailey Pavilion, Rockport 20
Barnes, Robert N. 151
Bascule Bridge 78, 79
Baychester 40
Bayview Hotel, Aransas Pass 19
Ben Grande Saloon 30
Benjamin, Ludy 122
Berlanga, Hugo 151
Bernhard, Alva 89
Blackout 90
Bostick, Ray 121
Breakers Hotel 136
Brendle Gin, Robstown 33
Brennan, Ed 61
Brother Leo 130
Bryan, William Jennings 22, 23

C
Cabaniss Field 96, 148
Caldwell Street Reservoir 67
Caller-Times 128-129
Camp Scurry 38-39
Cantu's Food Store 98
Censorship, World War II 91
Central Fire Station 87
Centre Theatre 92
Christmas lights on Chaparral 103
Circus parade on Chaparral 8
Clark's Watermelon Patch 82
Cliff Maus Field 51, 124-125
Cline's Landing 12
Collins, Bruce 101
Concrete ships, Port Aransas 45

Corpus Christi Aero Club 51
Corpus Christi & Interurban Railway 25
Corpus Christi Kids 6
Corpus Christi High School 7, 21, 27
Corpus Christi Transfer Co. 45
Cowboys 55

D
David Hirsch baseball team 46
Daylite ship 69
Dempsey, Jack 104
Dobie, J. Frank 116
Don Patricio Causeway 58
Driscoll, Clara 14
Driscoll Hotel 108
Driscoll, Robert 49
Dunn No. 2 and No. 6 56
Dunn Ranch, Padre Island 134
Duval County Courthouse 27

E
East, Alice Kleberg 113
East, Sarita Kenedy 130
Estelle, ferry 157, cover

F
Farley, Barney 62, 70
Flato, Charles Jr. 13
Foreword 4
Foster, Walter 76

G
Garcia, C.S. 122
Garcia, Hector P. and Clotilde 118
Garza, Reynaldo, Mr. and Mrs. 118
Garza, C.A. 122
Gipson, Fred 127
Glasscock, Gus 120
Goldthorn, Barney 107

H
Harte, Edward H. 129
Heinley, U.S. 25
Heldenfels Shipyard, Rockport 40
Herndon, Sydney 110
Herold, Victor Hugo 128

High Hat curb hops 86
Hirsch, Thomas 38
Homeseekers 24
Home Guard 94
Holly Beauty Salon 99
Hrissikopoulos, Charlie 100
Hunt, E. M. 122
Hurricane Beulah 133
Hurricane Carla 131-132
Hurricane Celia 137-143
Hurricane, 1916 32, 37
Heaney, Dr. A.G. 6

I, J
Ingleside Point 150
Jackrabbit on Shoreline 104
Jalisco Restaurant 93
Japonica 37
Johnson, Lady Bird 118, 135
Johnson, Lyndon B. 63, 106-107, 118
Jones, Luther (mayor) 151-152
Jones, Luther (lawyer) 145
Jones, W.W. 77

K
KC Barbecue Stand 71
King, Henrietta 113
King Ranch 112-115
Kingsville race track 66
Kleberg, Robert J. Jr. 112
Kleberg, Robert J. Sr. 113
KKK funeral 47
Knox, Frank 89

L
La Fruta Dam 119
Lagarto Bride 119
La Quinta 68
La Retama 77
Lerma Poultry-Eggs 54
Leopard Street 90
Ligon's Store 36
Longshoremen 127
Lozano, Gabe 34, 149

Old South Texas

Lozano's Groceries 34
Lozano, Vicente and Elvira 34
Luby, Jason 149

M Maddux, Jack 105
Marines, Company B 111
Maus, Cliff 51, 124
McCandless, Clarence 38
McDonald, Ben 118
McGregor, "Doc" 4, 116
McMahon, W. E. 122
McPherson, Aimee Semple 62
Metropolitan Café 47
Midway oil-field fire 57
Miller graduates 109
Miller, Roy 113
Miller, Maud (Heaney) 113
Mireles, Edmundo E. and Jovita 149
Misenhimer, Stokes 107
Missouri-Pacific depot 126
Moore, Harold 122
Municipal Wharf 73

N National Recovery Administration 64
Naval Air Station 89, 91, 96, 121
Nazi ship 81
Navy O&R Department 121
Nimitz parade 102
Noakes, New 101
North Beach 2, 32, 45, 52, 79, 80, 93, 101
Nueces Bay Causeway 42-43
Nueces County Courthouse, old 148

O Ocean Drive 26, 49, 72, 132
Ogontz freighter 49
Olympia Confectionery 100
Ortiz, Solomon 151
Oso Bridge washout 131
Oso Pier and Bait Stand 105

P Parr, Archer 146

Parr, Givens 107
Parr, George B. 103, 144-147
Pearl Harbor news 90
Peoples Street 75
Pig Stand No. 2 68
Pilot Boy 24
Pleasure Pier 59, 65
Poenisch, Herman & Bertha 33
Poenisch, Robert 14
Port Aransas Causeway 123
Port of Corpus Christi 48, 49, 78, 127
Portland Hotel 53
Princess Louise Hotel 76
Prohibition raids 60

Q, R Quintanilla-Perez, Selena 155
Rachal Ranch 41
Rainey, B.H. 122
Ranahan home 61
Resendez, Ramon Pena 153
Rhodes, Mary 156
Ritter, Robert 11
Ritz Theater 61
Rockport yacht basin 116
Rogers, Roy 105
Roosevelt, Franklin D. 70
Ross, Harold J. 52
Ruth, "Babe" 100

S Sailors at Aransas Pass 92
Sain, Hubert 107
Saltwater pool 101
San Antonio Machine Supply Co. 73
Sarita Mercantile Co. 68
Seaside Hotel 16, 17, 22, 23
Seawall 84-85
Second Texas Infantry team 39
Sinton Ladies Club 21
Sinton parade 66
South Texas Exposition 63
South Texas State Teachers College 44

St. Louis, Brownsville & Mexico Railroad 9
Stevenson, Coke 107
Swanter, Bob Sr. 59
Swinnea, O.F. 122

T Tarpon fishing 10, 35
Texas Star No. 3 97
Train Depot 31, 48, 122
Truan, Carlos 151

U Uehlinger, Marion 148
USS Borie 49
USS Lexington 154

W, Z Wallace, Mike 146
Water Street 72
Wells, Jim 114
White Point blowout 41
Wilson, Sam and Ada 110
Winerich Motors 87
Wyman, L. 122
Wynn Seale Junior High 67
Zackie's Playhouse Restaurant 83

Old South Texas

About the author

Murphy D. Givens is a native Texan, born in Gatesville, who grew up and attended public schools and college in Alabama. He worked as a reporter and editor at newspapers in Alabama, Michigan and Mississippi before joining the *Caller-Times* in 1981. He is the Viewpoints Editor, sits on the Editorial Board, and has written more than 200 columns on Corpus Christi and South Texas history. His radio commentary on local history airs each Friday on KEDT-FM. He is married and has two children.

Project staff

Murphy D. Givens, author
Fernando Ortiz Jr., designer
James Simmons, cover designer
Frank Lemos, project imager

Additional thanks to the following people who contributed photos or otherwise helped with this book:
Steve Arnold, *Caller-Times*; Bill Chriss; Joyce Dunn, South Texas Museum, Alice; Katherine Hrissikopoulos; Cecilia Aros Hunter, Texas A&M University-Kingsville; Stephanie K. Judjahn, Texas Maritime Museum, Rockport; Kevin Kerrigan, *Caller-Times*; Paul Madden, Quincy, Mass.; Margaret Neu, *Caller-Times*; Brooks Peterson, *Caller-Times*; Harriet Tillman; Ceil Venable; and William F. White.